FLUTE

Walt Disney Pictures Presents

THE LION KING

Original Songs
Music *by* Elton John
Lyrics *by* Tim Rice

A piano accompaniment book (HL00849955) is available for this collection.

ISBN 0-7935-3502-6

Artwork © The Walt Disney Company

HAL•LEONARD™
CORPORATION
7777 W. BLUEMOUND RD. P.O. BOX 13819 MILWAUKEE, WI 53213

CIRCLE OF LIFE

Music by ELTON JOHN
Lyrics by TIM RICE

Flute

I JUST CAN'T WAIT TO BE KING

Flute

Music by ELTON JOHN
Lyrics by TIM RICE

BE PREPARED

Music by ELTON JOHN
Lyrics by TIM RICE

Flute

HAKUNA MATATA

Music by ELTON JOHN
Lyrics by TIM RICE

FLUTE

Repeat ad lib. and Fade

CAN YOU FEEL THE LOVE TONIGHT

Music by ELTON JOHN
Lyrics by TIM RICE

FLUTE

CAN YOU FEEL THE LOVE TONIGHT

(as performed by ELTON JOHN)

Music by ELTON JOHN
Lyrics by TIM RICE

Flute

CIRCLE OF LIFE
(as performed by ELTON JOHN)

Music by ELTON JOHN
Lyrics by TIM RICE

FLUTE

I JUST CAN'T WAIT TO BE KING

(as performed by ELTON JOHN)

Music by ELTON JOHN
Lyrics by TIM RICE

Flute